Behavior-Based
Interview

Selecting the Right

Terry L. Fitzwa

A Crisp Fifty-Minute™ *Series Book*

This Fifty-Minute™ book is designed to be "read with a pencil." It is an excellent workbook for self-study as well as classroom learning. All material is copyright-protected and cannot be duplicated without permission from the publisher. *Therefore, be sure to order a copy for every training participant by contacting:*

THOMSON
COURSE TECHNOLOGY™

1-800-442-7477 • 25 Thomson Place, Boston MA • www.courseilt.com

Behavior-Based Interviewing

Selecting the Right Person for the Job

Terry L. Fitzwater

CREDITS:

Senior Editor: **Debbie Woodbury**
Editors: **Matthew A. Lusher; Charlotte Bosarge**
Production Manager: **Denise Powers**
Design: **Amy Shayne**
Production Artist: **Carol Lindahl, Liesel Lund**
Cover Design: **Nicole Phillips**

ISBN 1-56052-583-5
Library of Congress Catalog Card Number 00-104570
Printed in Canada by Webcom Limited

7 8 9 10 PM 06 05 04

Learning Objectives For:

BEHAVIOR-BASED INTERVIEWING

The objectives for *Behavior-Based Interviewing* are listed below. They have been developed to guide you, the reader, to the core issues covered in this book.

THE OBJECTIVES OF THIS BOOK ARE:

❑   1) To explain how to develop objective job criteria

❑   2) To provide a technique for developing objective, open-ended interview questions

❑   3) To teach how to conduct an objective interview that extracts in-depth information from the applicant

❑   4) To demonstrate how to analyze interview results and rate applicants against objective criteria

❑   5) To show how to follow up the interview process with rejection and offer letters

ASSESSING YOUR PROGRESS

In addition to the learning objectives above, Course Technology has developed a Crisp Series **assessment** that covers the fundamental information presented in this book. A 25-item, multiple-choice and true/false questionnaire allows the reader to evaluate his or her comprehension of the subject matter. To buy the assessment and answer key, go to www.courseilt.com and search on the book title or via the assessment format, or call 1-800-442-7477.

Assessments should not be used in any employee selection process.

Preface

Behavior-Based Interviewing is your guide to an interviewing methodology that will ensure consistency in the measurable areas of approach, research, design of questions, and ultimately a final hire or no-hire decision. The process allows interviewing by anyone, without the organization second-guessing what is stated in the interview. All you need to do is follow the process.

If you find yourself at the other end of the hiring process—as the job candidate—be sure to read the companion book to this one, *Preparing for the Behavior-Based Interview*. You may also want to use that book if you are in the position to mentor or coach those who are involved in a job search. Good luck, and "happy hiring!"

Terry L. Fitzwater

About the Author

Terry L. Fitzwater is a principal with Fitzwater Leadership Consulting with his principle office in California. He has authored three books in the Manager's Pocket Guide Series: *Preventing Sexual Harassment, Documenting Employee Performance,* and *Employee Relations.* He is also the author of a companion book to this one, *Preparing for the Behavior-Based Interview.* He is a frequent speaker and university instructor, and instructs on-site business classes in performance management, employee relations, and other topics.

He holds a bachelor's degree in business administration and a master's degree in human resources and organization development. You can contact him at 916-791-0692 or by email at tfitzh2o@quiknet.com.

Contents

Introduction

Phase 1: Gather Information

Phase 2: Conduct the Interview

Phase 3: Interpret Behavior

Phase 4: Follow-Up

Appendix A

Appendix B

INTRODUCTION

2

Introduction

When you think of selecting the right person for an open position, often your first inclination is to focus on the external hire—this is a natural leap considering that is where most organizations historically spend most of their time and energy. But in today's environment of empowerment and frequent organizational change, this focus must change. Selecting the right person for the right job is also something you will need to do for internal decisions such as promotions, forming teams and special task forces, and making other assignments.

Given the current pace of technological advances, it is not enough to hire a person based solely on what you *think* they can do. Behavioral, objective, fact-based selection criteria must be developed to increase your chance of placing the right person in the right job at the right time. The development of practical, specific, well-defined behavioral criteria will assist the manager and/or interviewer in determining if the person can deliver the expected results, as well as help you justify your placement decision legally, if necessary.

It has been said that the best predictor of future behavior (and success) is past successful behavior. In the employee selection process, that premise changes the focus. Now, an interview should not concentrate on what a prospective employee can do for you in the *future*, but rather on what has made that person successful *in the past*—and how can you best use those traits to deliver the future.

Past success is a predictor of future success

The Realities of Interviewing

66

70% felt the interviewees feel that the interview process is a strong indicator of how the company operates."

HR Magazine, **March 1998**

The selection process of any organization will send one of two messages to an applicant. One is a message of encouragement; one is a message of nonchalance or disregard for the candidate. A recent survey by *HR Magazine* supports the need for trained interviewers and professionalism. The survey results revealed:

➤ 39% of the respondents said their number one frustration was that interviewers were "not prepared and not focused during the interview."

➤ 38% of respondents were frustrated by a "lack of feedback on the status of their candidacy."

➤ 27% said they did not receive written position descriptions or that descriptions differed from one interviewer to another within the same company.

These responses send a clear message to any organization retooling or developing a behavior-based selection process. *Be attentive to the applicant*—it can be the difference between getting the candidate you want and losing a talented person to the competition.

SELF-ASSESSMENT: BEING ATTENTIVE TO THE APPLICANT

Consider these questions.

How often have you...

Sent the wrong message by leaving someone in the waiting room well past the scheduled interview time?

Kept the applicant waiting during the course of a day-long interview process?

Kept a candidate waiting because you returned to your office late?

Glanced at your watch or answered the telephone while conducting an interview?

Allowed your interview to be interrupted by someone tapping on your door?

While some will read this and think the above to be absurd behavior, the study by *HR Magazine* suggests it still exists to a large extent. The message sent by the respondents to this survey is clear—anyone involved in the interviewing process must be attentive and prepared, for not only is the company evaluating the candidate—the candidate is evaluating the company.

The Legalities of Interviewing

Lack of preparation is an accident waiting to happen and one no organization can afford. Interviewers must do whatever they can to eliminate the subjective nature of the interview process. Basing decisions on "gut" feel or giving in to biases—such as those against tattoos, long hair, rings in the nose—only add to the possibility of potentially expensive lawsuits, allegations of discriminatory practices, and ineffective selection decisions. It is imperative to develop objective criteria that every person is measured against equally.

An EEOC Perspective

How you conduct the interview is important. John Montoya, a former deputy director of the EEOC has stated that poor interview practices will prompt the agency to look very closely at an organization's recruitment practices. He sites four areas that bring EEOC scrutiny:

1. TESTING

Any test that is used whether written tests or tests for agility or performance should be validated. The agency will demand proof of validation.

2. INTERVIEW QUESTIONS

Complaints of disparate treatment are common in hiring cases and an employer must take steps to ensure all applicants are treated equally. *To prevent the impression of bias, you must ask all applicants the same set of prepared questions.*

3. INTERVIEW PANELS

The commission will look at the *make-up* of each panel in terms of race, sex, age, national origin, and disability.

4. INTERVIEW NOTES

Interviewers should avoid a tendency to write down *extraneous notes* about the way a person looks, dresses, grooms, or acts as opposed to notes specific to the job and the behaviors to be successful in the job.

EXERCISE: RATE YOUR INTERVIEWING FAIRNESS

How would you rate your skills and the hiring practices of your company against Mr. Montoya's list?

5=excellent	3=good	1=needs improvement

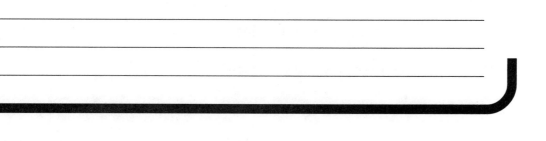

	Self	Company
Testing	5 4 3 2 1	5 4 3 2 1
Interview questions	5 4 3 2 1	5 4 3 2 1
Interview panels	5 4 3 2 1	5 4 3 2 1
Interview notes	5 4 3 2 1	5 4 3 2 1

Write down what particular behaviors you think are deficient in any of the areas above. As you go through the book, think about ways you can improve in these areas.

_____

_____

_____

The Behavior-Based Interview Process

This book provides a four-phase process to defining a consistent approach to interviewing and making hiring decisions.

PHASE 1: Gather Information

PHASE 2: Conduct the Interview

PHASE 3: Interpret Behavior

PHASE 4: Follow-Up

Each phase includes specific tasks for you to perform that lead to the final, ideal outcome: getting the right person in the right job at the right time. Following these steps will help determine whether the candidate possesses the skills, knowledge, and experience to perform the position. Along the way you will learn:

➤ The importance of research

➤ How to develop and write position descriptions and job-specific criteria

➤ The legalities of interviewing

➤ What to do after the interview

➤ Some additional effective interviewing tips and techniques

You will also learn how to prepare for the interview objectively—that is, establish an entire process dealing with measurable, objective, fact-based criteria—criteria that is *not* subjectively biased by your own personal preferences, opinions, and judgments.

The Four-Phase Selection Model

You can use this form as a checklist as you complete each task.

Phase 1: Gather Information

- ❏ Review position descriptions
- ❏ Review performance appraisals
- ❏ Discuss with those who have knowledge of the position (Knowledge Givers)
- ❏ Develop job-related success criteria
- ❏ Review requisition form
- ❏ Review and compare the applicant's background and other credentials versus job-related criteria

Phase 2: Conduct the Interview

- ❏ Develop interview questions
- ❏ Script the interview
- ❏ Set the interview parameters with the candidate
- ❏ Ask open-ended questions
- ❏ Probe the answers for detail and clarification
- ❏ Gather job-related information from interview
- ❏ Observe and document job-related behavioral data

Phase 3: Interpret Behavior

- ❏ Analyze and interpret notes
- ❏ Evaluate behaviors against criteria
- ❏ Evaluate behaviors against a norm
- ❏ Assign a rating
- ❏ Make a decision

Phase 4: Follow-Up

- ❏ Post interview follow-up
- ❏ Offer/reject letter

10

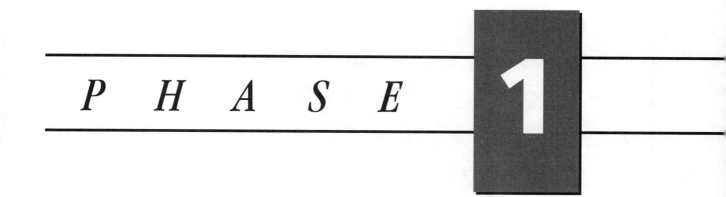

PHASE 1

Gather

Information

12

The Behavior-Based Interview

The behavior-based interview begins with research and the search for fact-based information. This may include documents such as:

➤ the Employee Requisition Form

➤ the Position Description

➤ information from those who currently hold, have held, or manage the position

➤ past Performance Reviews of the candidate

Combined, these sources will paint a picture of the position requirements and establish a profile of desired skills, abilities, knowledge, and experience that the ideal candidate will possess. This information will be needed later to develop and frame interview questions and help avoid the interview syndrome of "ready, fire, aim."

The Employee Requisition Form

The Employee Requisition Form is the first of the documents to research. The form is used in many organizations to justify the hiring of new personnel. Here is a typical form:

XYZ Corporation
Employee Requisition Form

Position Title:_____ **Reports to:**_____

Salary Range:_____ **Date:**_____

- ❐ Additional Headcount
- ❐ Replacement
- ❐ Budget
- ❐ Non-Budgeted

Essential Duties: Detail key position requirements

Essential Qualifications: Detail education and experience

Replacement/Addition Justification: Detail the need for replacement at this time and funding

_____ _____ _____
Completed by **Department/Function Head** **Human Resources**

The focus of this document will be to define the *essential duties* and *essential qualifications* of the job. When properly completed, both sections of this document will give considerable insight into recruitment specifics.

Essential Duties

For example, the essential duties section for a human resources manager may look like this:

Essential Duties: Detail key position requirements

✔ Ability to work comfortably at all levels of the organization

✔ Direct all strategic Human Resources (HR) activities

✔ Develop and administer all compensation and benefit plans

✔ Design employee relations strategies to minimize unionization, harassment charges, charges of discrimination, and wrongful discharge lawsuits.

This information leads you to a more comprehensive conclusion: the need for a seasoned human resource professional, a strategic thinker, a good communicator at all organizational levels, well-versed in employment law, and familiar with the design, not just administration, of compensation and benefit plans.

Think about your own position in your company. In the blank below, list the essential duties of your own position.

Essential Duties: Detail key position requirements

The Employee Requisition Form (CONTINUED)

Essential Qualifications

Essential Qualifications: Detail education and experience

✔ A graduate degree in HR

✔ 15+ years experience in HR

✔ Generalist familiar with all aspects of HR work

✔ SPHR (Senior Professional in HR certification)

This additional information begins to focus the picture and adds a great deal more insight into the specific qualifications of the ideal candidate. One can immediately discern a need to eliminate any individual without the requisite degree, training, and certification.

In the blank below, list the essential qualifications of your own position.

Essential Qualifications: Detail education and experience

The Position Description

The Position Description usually consists of multiple sections, including:

1. **Heading.** The actual title of the job, who the employee reports to, the location of the position, and the date.

2. **Basic Functions.** One to three sentences describing the end result expected from the position. It will describe the job's relationship to both corporate and/or business unit objectives—i.e., why the position exists.

3. **Dimensions.** Summarizes the quantitative job data most relevant to the position (i.e., technical ability). Select the factors most closely-related and clearly-impacted.

4. **Organization.** Details other positions reporting to this position. Often an organization chart is attached for clarification.

5. **Nature and Scope.** A one-paragraph description of the business environment in which the position is performed.

6. **Key Accountabilities/Responsibilities.** Describes the major components of the position. Specifically lists each element of the major accountabilities/responsibilities and essential job functions.

7. **Education and Experience Requirements.** Briefly describes the education and experience the incumbent must possess to be totally effective in this position.

8. **Physical Context/Work Environment.** Describes the physical context in which the essential job functions are performed.

9. **Other Special Skills/Certifications/Abilities.**

The information contained in the Position Description usually overlaps the Employee Requisition Form and serves to both reemphasize and confirm specific needs. The Position Description itself can be used internally or externally. As an example, it is an excellent piece of information to give external search agencies who are conducting searches of behalf of your organization.

Look at a Position Description for a human resources manager to add further definition to your dimensions and to illustrate how the documents come together. Keep in mind as you read the Position Description that it describes the position, *not the person*, for which the information is gathered.

The Position Description (CONTINUED)

XYZ Corporation
Position Description (Sample)

Heading:

Title: Manager of Human Resources
Reports to: President
Location: Tampa, Florida
Date of Preparation: July 13 (year)

Basic Function:

The position provides direction, guidance, and support on all human resource policies, procedures, and practices. It further provides for compliance with all federal, state, and local laws and regulations to achieve fulfillment of all corporate and divisional human resource objectives.

Dimensions:

	Measurement:	Amount impacted/controlled:
Dimension 1:	2000 employees	Total wages: 150mm
Dimension 2:	Benefit management	6 plans-total budget 50mm
Dimension 3:	Staff development	2mm budget

Supervision of others:

	Direct reports:	Indirect reports:
# required:	7	17
# of exempt	5	2
# of non-exempt/hourly	1	n/a

Travel required: 25% (domestic and international)

Organization:

Titles: The supervisors of compensation and benefits, employee relations, training and development, staffing, and three plant HR managers.

Position Description Form, continued

Nature and Scope:

XYZ is a developer, manufacturer, and distributor of widget equipment and ancillaries. The company is headquartered in Tampa, Florida with 12 distribution centers located around the world. The total sales of the organization is $900mm with an associated workforce of 2000 employees.

Key Accountabilities and Responsibilities:

(1) Staff development (2) Strategic HR planning (3) Maintaining the company's non-union status (4) Develop and administer all compensation and benefit plans to ensure competitiveness in the marketplace (5) Continually assess staffing levels to ensure proper levels (6) Handle all legal complaints and bring to a successful conclusion.

Education and Experience Requirements:

This position requires a seasoned HR professional with a minimum of 15 years HR experience in a manufacturing environment. International experience in the Benelux countries and Japan is preferred. A graduate degree in Organization Development (OD) is a must.

Physical Context/Work Environment:

Work is typically conducted in an office environment. However, frequent travel both domestically and internationally requires frequent walking or some ability to move about quickly.

Other Special Skills/Certifications/Abilities:

SPHR certification

Disclaimer: This information is intended to describe the general nature, level of the position and the level of work, and should not be construed as an exhaustive list of all duties, responsibilities, and skills required for the position.

Information provided by: _____ **Date:** _____

Information reviewed by: _____ **Date:** _____

The Position Description (CONTINUED)

What has creating this additional form provided? The knowledge that the position requires, in addition to those noted from the requisition form, the following:

1. manufacturing experience

2. an advanced degree in Organizational Development

3. ability to travel

4. international experience

5. major budget responsibilities

Later, this same information will be used to develop interview dimensions from which you will base your behavior-based interview questions.

Consulting with Knowledge Givers

The final information-gathering phase is discussing the open position with those who know the position: people who have held it before, hold it now, or supervise it now. The goal is to find out as much as possible about the position's key duties, responsibilities, and educational requirements that the information review cannot uncover. As an example: Who does the position interact with and at what levels? What personality type best fits with those already in the department or with those who interact with the position?

You can gain other additional and invaluable insights from Knowledge Givers through the use of a two tools:

➤   a Current and Future-Based Questionnaire

➤   a Competency Scale

Creating and using these tools will help you determine other success criteria for the position you need to fill.

Consulting with Knowledge Givers (CONTINUED)

Complete this form for your own position to give you an idea of its use.

Current and Future-Based Questionnaire
Determining Additional Skills

Define the position's current management skill sets:

How will strategic and/or operating plans or conditions change or modify those skills?

Define the position's current technical skill sets:

How will strategic and/or operating plans or conditions change or modify those skills?

What factors make someone successful?

Will those factors change over time?

Are there any new and emerging technologies applicable to this position?

Notice the questions ask for two conclusions:

1. What makes someone successful now?

2. Will conditions change or modify over time, requiring new
    and/or improved skills?

This exercise will pay off in the additional interview questions we will
develop from it. The questions will lead a search effort now focused on the
future as well as the present.

USING A COMPETENCY SCALE

There is another method to use to measure the current and future importance of a behavior or skill. While interviewing the Knowledge Givers, have them score skills and behaviors using the following form:

Competency Scale

Score each of the following behaviors and/or skills using this scale.

5=very important	3=neutral	1=not important

"Future" is defined as three to five years from now.

	Current Importance	Future Importance
Delegation	5 4 3 2 1	5 4 3 2 1
Coaching	5 4 3 2 1	5 4 3 2 1
Strategic thinking	5 4 3 2 1	5 4 3 2 1
Risk taking	5 4 3 2 1	5 4 3 2 1
Leadership	5 4 3 2 1	5 4 3 2 1

In this example, say someone rated delegation as currently a 2, but in the future rates it a 5. This would tell you that although this behavior is not important now, with the changes the person sees in the future, it will become a very important skill. This knowledge will enable the development of interview questions uniquely important in the interview. In this example, some of the questions will need to focus on the person's ability to delegate. Use this format with your own organization's competencies for maximum effectiveness.

The Performance Review

Most performance reviews have two sections important to fact-based research: a section for the "strengths" of the employee and a section for the "developmental needs" of the employee. A careful review of past performance reviews for those who have held the position may confirm your findings from the Employee Requisition and Position Description forms and will often offer new insights. (Note: For privacy reasons, *do not* review performance reviews without the permission of the employee.) As an example, look at a section dealing with the developmental needs for a human resource professional.

Developmental Needs: Dennis Kline

Dennis has great interpersonal skills; however, he needs to better manage his time. While his style is to manage by walking around, it is taking too much time away from his other duties sometimes resulting in missed deadlines. Dennis needs to prioritize his time in such a manner that he gets his work done before socialization.

Your research to this point has yielded several additional bits of information. First, it confirms something you found earlier—the need for interpersonal skills. However, it introduces a new criteria: time management. And, in a human resources position—one responsible for a division with domestic and international responsibilities—this information is not surprising. This and anything else you find useful will be added to the final Position Requirements/Profile.

The Position Requirements/Profile

Your research efforts have resulted in a vast array of skills that are "musts" for the position you are trying to fill. This information is used to develop a Position Requirements/Profile. Look again at the sample human resource position on pages 15, 16, 22, and 24 and check (✔) your findings against this Position Requirements/Profile. Here is what you know as a result of your research.

Position Requirements/Profile

❑ Ability to work comfortably at all levels of the organization

❑ Ability to think and direct strategically

❑ Ability to design and administer all compensation and benefit plans

❑ Ability to design employee relations strategies to minimize unionization, harassment charges/claims, charges of discrimination, and wrongful discharge lawsuits

❑ Graduate degree in Organizational Development

❑ 5+ years of experience in a manufacturing environment

❑ Generalist familiar with all HR disciplines

❑ SPHR certification

❑ Ability to travel

❑ International experience

❑ Fiduciary experience with knowledge and use of budgets

❑ Time management

To construct objective, job-related, behavior-based interview questions, you need to compare it against a standard glossary of defined behaviors, a list of work behaviors with company-specific definitions. As you review each definition on the following pages, compare the definition against your organization. Make appropriate changes if necessary by writing over the term and adding your own.

GLOSSARY OF DEFINED BEHAVIORS

Administrative skills: identifies tasks and reaches goals as a logical sequence.

Analytical: assimilates data/variables and brings to a reasoned conclusion.

Business acumen: understanding the entire business, not just functional expertise.

Business partnering: ability to partner/interact with others at all levels.

Coaching: continual, constructive, ongoing feedback/advice.

Communications: ability to make a point whether oral or written.

Counseling: providing career and personal advise for growth and development

Creativity: ability to devise/create alternatives without a road map.

Customer service: understands the importance of internal and external customer relations.

Decision making: ability to make timely/quality decisions not necessarily with all the information needed.

Delegation: the assigning of tasks and objectives to others.

Dimension: terminology expressing a broad view of a behavior or skill. (See 200 questions at the end of the book for 20 defined dimensions.)

Education: necessary education/credentials/training for a task/position.

Facilitation: ability to lead a group in idea generation.

Influence: tactful discussion with others to change a view or guide to a conclusion other than their own.

Initiative: does whatever it takes to deliver results without waiting for instructions.

Innovation: creates new solutions to varying situations, tasks, problems.

Interpersonal skills: ability to relate/communicate/empathize with at all levels of the organization.

Leadership: demonstrates by example a willingness to be out in front.

Listening skills: receives/hears the entire message before speaking or formulating a response.

Managing change: views and welcomes change as necessary for people and organizational growth and improvement.

Glossary of Defined Behaviors (CONTINUED)

Mentoring: guiding and directing for the purpose of development/success.

Motivational skills: ability to get others to give their best to organizational goals/objectives.

Negotiation skills: ability to formulate and discuss plan/alternatives with others to reach agreement.

People development: ability to teach or provide the skills needed for task achievement.

Potential behavior: behavioral subsets within a dimension that give definition to the dimension and the skills required for success.

Problem identification: ability to see/anticipate troublesome issues and recommend resolution/solutions.

Process improvement: continually looks for a better way; not satisfied with the status quo.

Quality orientation: never takes short cuts at the expense of doing things right.

Resourceful: seeks alternative strategies, materials, people, and products.

Results orientation: delivers tasks/assignments on time, every time.

Risk taking: views failure as an opportunity for growth despite personal risk or exposure.

Strategic thinking: continually assessing the future for potential.

Team formation: supports team concept and selects appropriate chemistry mix/talents.

Technical skills: requisite knowledge and expertise for the task/function.

Time management: the optimum, efficient use of time to maximize the results of self and others.

Add any others used frequently by your organization:

_____

_____

_____

_____

There are more behaviors and many organizations have them similarly profiled. This piece of the selection process will have a greater chance of adding meaningful data when it is coupled with organization-specific terminology and definitions. Add this list to yours for maximum effectiveness.

Creating a Dimension Matrix

Based upon the information you have gathered in Phase 1, you will now create a *Dimension Matrix*. A Dimension Matrix is an easy-to-use, three-column form.

The best way to understand the distinctions between the three columns is to look at an example using the human resources position.

Dimension	Behavior-Based Findings	Potential Behavior
Technical:	-HR generalist -Compensation and benefits experience /expertise -Knowledge of employment law -15+ years of experience	-Problem Identification -Administrative Skills -Technical Skills -Analytical Skills
Education:	-Masters in OD -SPPHR Certification	-Education
Interpersonal:	-Ability to work at all levels	-Customer Service -Influence -Listening -Facilitation Skills -Negotiation Skills
Business Acumen:	-Fiduciary skills -Strategic thinker -Internationl experience	-Leadership -Business Partnering -Strategic Thinking -Managing Change
Managerial Skills:	-Composite	-Delegation -Coach -Mentor -People Development -Resourceful -Process Improvement -Motivational Skills

Creating a Dimension Matrix (CONTINUED)

The three columns contain the following information:

Dimensions: general categories of qualification

Behavior-based findings: particular skills within those categories

Potential behaviors: specific job behaviors that requires or exemplifies those behavior-based skills

Each dimension establishes a core competency required for the position. As an example, business acumen (a dimension) is defined as a skill to think strategically on a global basis—a behavior-based finding. The last column, potential behaviors, is the determination of behaviors needed within the category taken from the Glossary of Defined Behaviors on page 27.

When developing dimensions it is best to limit the number. Too many dimensions will dilute your interviewing effort. The goal is to focus your limited interviewing time on the candidate's qualifications and whether he/she is a fit for the open position. Try it for your own position: fill out the grid based on the dimensions, behavior-based findings, and potential behaviors of someone doing your job.

Dimension	Behavior-Based Findings	Potential Behavior

Background Review

The final stage of Phase 1 is to review each applicant's background against the information you have compiled. Compare the "Position Requirements/Profile" you have created to the applicant's resume or application. Since a position requirements/profile form is very detailed, it is easy to determine if the applicant has the desired skills and experience. As an example, the applicant either has international experience or not. The applicant either has 15+ years of experience or not. If the comparison meets your needs, it is time to prepare for the interview and move to the information phase. However, always remember that you may choose to interview someone who *almost* meets the criteria. As an example, you may decide to interview a person with 10 years of experience, not the expected 15, since that person has the applicable international experience.

32

Conduct the

Interview

Principles of Effective Interviewing

Developing the most effective interview questions—those that determine the applicant's skill levels compared to the position's requirements—takes time. As you prepare for the interview, remember these basic principals:

➤ The best predictor of future behavior and potential success is past actual behavior and tangible deliverables.

➤ Fact-based preparation increases the likelihood of an interview that is focused on skills and abilities to do the job.

➤ Questions should always focus on job-related issues/tasks.

➤ Assessment accuracy is always increased when several sources of information and trained interviewers are used.

➤ If the interview is conducted in a professional manner it increases the chances that the applicant will accept the job, if offered.

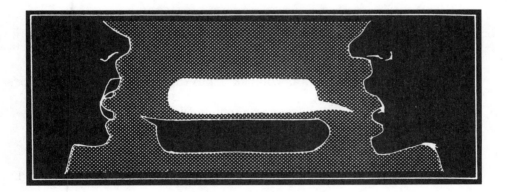

Developing Interview Questions

Interview questions derive naturally from the pre-work accomplished in the preparation phase. The information gathered will make it easy to create another matrix of dimensions for the position.

There are several reasons why creating interview questions prior to the interview is not a waste of time:

1. Scripting the interview will ensure each person involved in the actual interviews understands the position and what is required of the position. In effect, everyone is "singing off the same sheet of music."

2. Scripting will keep the interviewer focused. This will help avoid the occasional "stray" question that could be construed as illegal by the applicant. (More on this in a moment.) Per the EEOC's caution, this is especially important when multiple interviewers are involved.

3. Scripting lets the interviewee know that the company takes the process seriously and thoroughly researched backgrounds before initiating interviews. *Remember, not only is the company evaluating the applicant, the applicant is evaluating the company.*

Non-scripted Questions

On occasion, the applicant's responses will force you to follow up with questions not on your script. If this happens:

1. Make sure the question you ask is job-related. If the question does not relate to the job, do not ask it.

2. Jot down each non-scripted question as you asked it. This will document the question should disagreements as to content and purpose surface after the interview. As remote as this may sound, you never know what a rejected candidate might do.

The Interview Question Matrix

The questions you develop must align with the Dimension Matrix developed for the job on page 29. This example matrix includes five dimensions:

➤ Technical

➤ Education

➤ Interpersonal

➤ Business acumen

➤ Managerial skills

Each dimension is further defined from the Position Requirements/Profile and the Glossary of Defined Behaviors. Now you need to ask, "What questions can we ask to discover behaviors identified with each dimension?"

Look at the first dimension, Technical, as an example:

Dimension	Behavior-Based Findings	Potential Behavior
Technical:	-HR generalist -Compensation and benefits experience /expertise -Knowledge of employment law -15+ years of experience	-Problem Identification -Administrative Skills -Technical Skills -Analytical Skills

Questions to elicit behavior and confirm dimension requirements.

1. Define your experience as a generalist and discuss all of the HR disciplines with which you have expertise.
2. Describe your experience as it pertains to developing compensation and benefit plans.
3. Describe a situation where your knowledge of employment law was used.
4. This position requires that you handle multiple tasks. Describe a situation where that was the case and how you prioritized those tasks.
5. Describe a situation where you had to deal with a complex set of issues and how you resolved them.
6. Are there any areas where you feel your expertise is lacking and if so what are they and how can they be strengthened?
7. What new and emerging HR technologies do you plan on using in the next five years?

The Interview Question Matrix (CONTINUED)

What you should notice is that each question directly relates to the technical dimension and its corresponding behavior-based findings and potential behavior. The answers given by the applicants will determine their capabilities within the dimension. The interviewer will note the answers on a form introduced next. But, first look at another example, Education.

Dimension	Behavior-Based Findings	Potential Behavior
Education:	-Master's in OD -SPHR Certification	-Education

Questions to elicit behavior and confirm dimension requirements.

1. Do you have a Master's degree and if so what is it in?
2. Do you have an SPHR certification?
3. What inspired you to return to school for the Master's?
4. What inspired you to seek the SPHR certification?
5. Do you have other degrees or certifications that you feel are of benefit to this position and if so what are they and why do you see them as important?

It is understood that in the education category most resumés will show the applicant's educational background. If not, the above questions are most appropriate. However, if a Master's degree is listed, your question will change slightly. You could combine question number one with question number three to ask, "I see you have a Master's Degree in OD; what inspired you to return to school for the Master's?"

Here is an example using the Managerial Skills dimension:

Dimension	Behavior-Based Findings	Potential Behavior
Managerial Skills:	-Composite	-Delegation -Coach -Mentor -People Development -Resourceful -Process Improvement -Motivational Skills

Questions to elicit behavior and confirm dimension requirements.

1. Give me examples of how you have developed your staff to assume positions of greater responsibility.

2. Give me examples of methodologies you have changed or added to improve process flow.

3. If you feel that someone is not performing up to their capabilities, how do you get them to achieve their potential?

4. Give me an example of a problem, issue, or concern that you handled in a unique, creative way.

5. Give me an example of a recent performance review where you listed some development needs and how you worked with the person to develop an improvement plan.

6. Tell me about some of the people you have worked with who later became successful and what you did to contribute to that success.

7. Give me an example of a major crisis and the person you assigned to the crisis to fix it. What was the end result?

In each of the above examples, the questions were developed in a few minutes. It was easy to develop question number six, in the above example, knowing that a required potential behavior of the Manager of Human Resources position is *people development.*

The strength of formatting the interview based upon job requirements is this: anyone can conduct the interview because the process has been established on a purely *objective* basis. For example, it does not require an HR professional to assess an HR candidate because the interviewer is assessing *fact-based skills only*; for instance, delegation, people development, and so on.

The Interview Question Matrix (CONTINUED)

Using the Matrix

Most interviewers can use the matrix tools even if they are interviewing outside their area of expertise or discipline. All an interviewer needs to know is what skills and/or behaviors need to be assessed, given the position. Use the material you have gathered so far to develop interview questions.

Dimension	Behavior-Based Findings	Potential Behavior

Questions to elicit behavior and confirm dimension requirements.

The Importance of Questions

Think of the entire interview process as a vacation. You would not think of
jumping into your car and driving across the country without a road map or a
plan. You have to know where you are going in order to arrive at the destination;
the same is true for the selection interview. You cannot know if your applicant is
qualified without asking the right questions. The behavior-based interview
process is the road map to making objective, fact-based hiring decisions.

The Importance of Questions (CONTINUED)

Legal versus Illegal Questions

Before you begin preparing your interview questions, it is important to understand the concept of legal versus illegal (or ill-conceived) questions. Sometimes there is a very fine line separating the two. Take the following quiz to determine how much you currently know about asking questions during an interview.

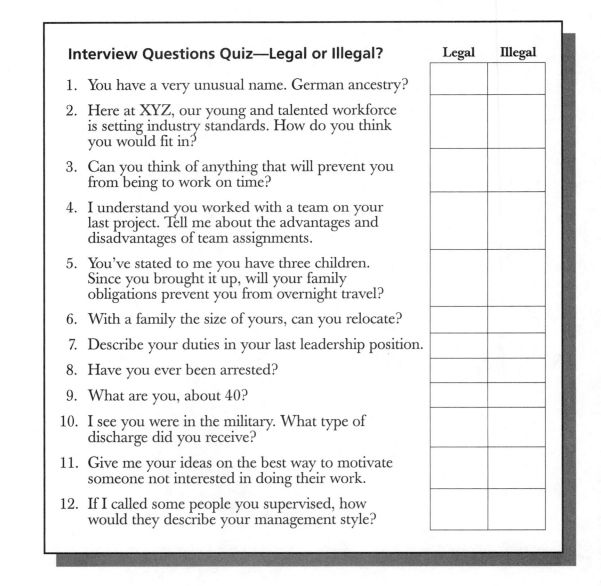

Interview Questions Quiz—Legal or Illegal? | Legal | Illegal |

1. You have a very unusual name. German ancestry?

2. Here at XYZ, our young and talented workforce is setting industry standards. How do you think you would fit in?

3. Can you think of anything that will prevent you from being to work on time?

4. I understand you worked with a team on your last project. Tell me about the advantages and disadvantages of team assignments.

5. You've stated to me you have three children. Since you brought it up, will your family obligations prevent you from overnight travel?

6. With a family the size of yours, can you relocate?

7. Describe your duties in your last leadership position.

8. Have you ever been arrested?

9. What are you, about 40?

10. I see you were in the military. What type of discharge did you receive?

11. Give me your ideas on the best way to motivate someone not interested in doing their work.

12. If I called some people you supervised, how would they describe your management style?

Compare your responses to the answer key on page 44.

Topics to Avoid

- ✔ **Arrests or police records.** Avoid questions concerning arrests. Some job-related questions are permitted concerning convictions, e.g., a conviction for embezzlement might disqualify a person for a position of financial analyst.

- ✔ **Sex.** Avoid any question that deal with the gender of the candidate (also see child care below).

- ✔ **Disability.** Avoid questions that deal with disability, e.g., extreme obesity.

- ✔ **Age.** Avoid questions that ask for the age of the applicant.

- ✔ **Military Service.** Avoid questions that ask the type of discharge.

- ✔ **Race/Color.** Avoid questions concerning skin color, hair type, eye color, or race.

- ✔ **Child Care.** Avoid asking how someone will care for a child or whether a person plans to have a family.

- ✔ **Religion.** Avoid questions that ask religious preference.

- ✔ **National Origin.** Avoid questions regarding birthplace, native language, or ancestry.

- ✔ **Marital Status.** Avoid questions concerning marriage.

Remember: Rejections should only be made for quantifiable job-related reasons.

The Importance of Questions (CONTINUED)

"Bona Fide Occupational Qualification"

There are, however, some exceptions regarding the legality of certain interview questions. Generally speaking, these exceptions are covered by the doctrine of *bona fide occupational qualification*. As an example, an organization may refuse to employ a female for a male rest room attendant. Or, an organization can refuse employment to a female if the position requires a male to model a gender-specific line of clothing.

Asking Questions

One final point, a skilled interviewer will be able to ask almost any question given proper preparation. As an example:

If the ability to travel is a requirement for the position, you could ask:

"This position requires a great deal of travel time, approximately 30%. Is this a concern for you?" or, "This position requires you to travel at least 30% of the time; is this an issue?"

You would *not* ask:

"I see you have children at home. How can you travel as required with such obligations?"

ANSWER KEY FOR INTERVIEW QUESTIONS QUIZ

Most illegal or ill-conceived questions deal with race, sex, color, religion, national origin, disability, and/or age. In the previous self-assessment, these question #s may be illegal for the following reasons:

1. Concerns nationality.
2. Concerns age.
5. Concerns child care.
6. Concerns family.
8. Concerns arrests.
9. Concerns age.
10. Concerns military discharge.

Always remember to keep personal questions out of the interview process. Keep the following handy as you plan the interview.

COMPOSING PROPER INTERVIEW QUESTIONS

All it takes is a little practice, a little thought, and an interview plan. Begin practicing by rewriting the questions below.

Question 1: "You've stated to me that you have three children. Since you brought it up, will your family obligations prevent you from traveling overnight?"

_____

_____

_____

Question 2: "With a family the size of yours can you relocate?"

_____

_____

_____

Question 3: "Will your disability prevent you from moving materials between conveyor belts?"

_____

_____

_____

Possible rewrites: (If factual)

Question 1: "This position sometimes requires travel at a moment's notice. Is this a concern and why?"

Question 2: "Ours is an organization that promotes from within. This normally means relocation. Is this a concern and why?"

Question 3: "This position requires the lifting of 100 pound material from one conveyor belt to another. Is there anything to keep you from compliance?"

Open-Ended and Closed Questions

The interviewer's task is to ask questions that not only challenge the interviewee but also *elicit a measurable response*. This is accomplished through the use of "open-ended" as opposed to "closed" questions. Open-ended questions begin with words like "Describe" or, "Tell me about…" They are effective because they require more than a "yes" or "no" response. A "yes" or "no" response to a closed question generates little valuable information unless it is followed by an open-ended question.

IDENTIFYING OPEN AND CLOSED QUESTIONS

Check (✔) if the following are open-ended or closed questions.

	Open	Closed
1. Tell me about your last supervisory position. Detail for me your duties and responsibilities.	❏	❏
2. Do you like to supervise?	❏	❏
3. Describe your management style.	❏	❏
4. Would you say that you have a democratic management style?	❏	❏
5. Have you ever had to discipline an employee? If so, describe the process for me.	❏	❏

Questions #1 and #3 are open-ended since they require explanation. Questions #2 and #4 are closed since they can be answered with a "yes," or a "no," or a one-word response. Question #5 starts with a closed question but ends with an open-ended question.

Probing

Another key interviewing skill is a technique called *probing*. It is nothing more than asking one or more clarifying questions concerning something that has been said by the candidate. For example:

Interviewer: *"Tell me about a difficult employee relations situation and how you dealt with it."*

Response: *"I once had an employee who accused a co-worker of sexual harassment."*

Interviewer: *(Probe) "Sounds difficult. What steps did you take to clear up the situation?"*

Probing continues until the interviewer is satisfied with the response or understands the situation.

Probe when you:

➤ receive an incomplete response

➤ detect avoidance of a response

➤ need additional information

➤ do not understand a response

Probing Techniques

1. **Paraphrase**
   Example: "If I heard you correctly here is what you said."

2. **Pause for effect**
   Example: Say nothing to force a further response.

3. **Directed feedback**
   Example: "So, you were the lead on that project?"

4. **Non-verbal**
   Example: Nodding, hand gestures, smiling, quizzical look.

The Interview Worksheet

Formatting an Interview Worksheet will also provide direction and a smooth transition from one part of the interview to another.

Here is the front page of the interview form:

**Interview
Worksheet**

Applicant's Name:_____

Interviewer's Name:_____

Position:_____

Date:_____

Note: Finalize notes/comments immediately following interview

The Interview Worksheet (CONTINUED)

Here is the reverse side of the Interview Worksheet. Expand or shrink the columns to fit your specific needs. (see Appendix B)

Behavior-Based Dimensions	Questions	Observable Behaviors/Notes

Rating:

❏ Acceptable   ❏ Acceptable with reservations   ❏ Unacceptable

Recommendations:

The first column, *Behavior-Based Dimensions*, lists the qualifications for the position. For the HR position it is technical, education, interpersonal, business acumen, and managerial skills. In the second column, *Questions*, you will write down interview questions developed for each dimension. In the third column, you will record *Observable Behaviors* and applicant responses to the questions. In the second section, *Rating*, you should develop a rating scale that is easy to use and can be used consistently by all interviewers. For example, you might use a numeric system: 5=superior, 3=good, 1=unacceptable. The final section, *Recommendations*, is used to document any additional comments or thoughts. Use the recommendations section to record final comments from the interviewer. Comments might include: "The candidate is acceptable to me. I am passing him/her along to the next person to interview." Or, "The candidate does not possess all of the skills needed to perform the position as noted." The key to this section is to keep your comments brief and *job-related*.

Here is an example of a completed worksheet.

Behavior-Based Dimensions	Questions	Observable Behaviors/Notes
Technical	What technical, etc.	Goal Oriented: Went back to school after 10 years to get Master's

Rating: 3

☑ Acceptable   ❑ Acceptable with reservations   ❑ Unacceptable

Recommendations:
Applicant is acceptable and I am passing her along for further interviews and additional assessment.

Notice that the observable behavior is *goal orientation*. The conclusion was confirmed by the applicant's return to college after a number of years to obtain a Master's degree. This is an example of the thought process and documentation needed by an interviewer to justify the conclusion of goal orientation. Many times in an interview you will form opinions, but the interview is never complete until you can justify each conclusion you draw by what is *stated* or *displayed* by the candidate.

Behavioral Rating Profile

The Behavioral Rating Profile is another method to use to rate the interviewee's behavior using the Glossary of Defined Behaviors on page 27. It simplifies the process and uses important material researched and defined in Phases 1 and 2. This format also lends itself to easy scoring during and after the interview. When you see the behavior, circle the appropriate rating.

Behavioral Rating Profile

Rating Scale:

5= Observable/Quantifiable   1= Not Apparent/Quantifiable

Delegation	5	4	3	2	1
Coaching	5	4	3	2	1
Mentoring	5	4	3	2	1
Strategic Thinking	5	4	3	2	1
Business Acumen	5	4	3	2	1
People Development	5	4	3	2	1
Risk Taking	5	4	3	2	1
Communications	5	4	3	2	1
Education	5	4	3	2	1
Creativity	5	4	3	2	1
Counseling	5	4	3	2	1
Problem Identification	5	4	3	2	1
Customer Service	5	4	3	2	1
Team Formation	5	4	3	2	1
Leadership Skills	5	4	3	2	1

The Interview Process

The interview process begins with the pre-screening interview. You can usually do this with a telephone call, or if you have the time, conduct a pre-screening interview face-to-face. In a telephone screening, all you are trying to do is verify the applicant's resumé statements. Does he/she really have the degrees listed? Does he/she really have the number of years experienced as outlined?

Keep this in mind as you conduct the interview: *what you do not see can hurt you.* Facial expressions and other attitudes and demeanors are impossible to detect over the wire. Your greatest opportunity to measure the tangible and the intangible is in a face-to-face conversation, as outlined next.

The On-Site Interview

There are five steps to follow to a construct a solid, well-focused interview.

Step 1: Introductions

Script the session

❏ Set interview guidelines and parameters
❏ Put the candidate at ease
❏ Detail the events of the day

Step 2: Interviewer Q&A

Record the session

❏ Ask questions from prepared spreadsheet
❏ Follow the 80/20 rule
❏ Record behaviors and responses

Step 3: Applicant Q&A

Equalize the session

❏ Entertain questions from the applicant

Step 4: Close

End the session

❏ Ask any remaining questions
❏ Facilitate next portion of the process
❏ Sell or dismiss

Step 5: Administrate

Document the session

❏ Analyze and interpret notes
❏ Hire/no hire decision

The Interview Process (CONTINUED)

Step 1: Introductions

There is nothing more disconcerting to an applicant than being left in the dark concerning the flow of the interview. The applicant is probably nervous, so anything that can be done to put the person at ease is a must. Scripting the interview—that is, describing the process—will assist in breaking down barriers and opening unfiltered communication channels.

RATING YOUR INTRODUCTION SKILLS

Here's a checklist to follow before moving to Step 2. Rate yourself as you read.

5=excellent	3=good	1=needs improvement

My rating:

❏ **Put the applicant at ease with small talk, offering a cup of coffee, soft drink, etc.**　　5 4 3 2 1

❏ **Set interview guideline and parameters**　　5 4 3 2 1
- ➤ expected length of the interview
- ➤ note taking
- ➤ process
- ➤ working from notes

❏ **Detail events of the day**　　5 4 3 2 1

Any items for which you rated yourself a 3 or lower deserve special attention. Focus on improving these introduction skills next time you interview job applicants.

Easing into the interview with small talk or sharing a cup of coffee will help take the "edge" off of the process. This naturally leads to a discussion where the rest of the process can be explained.

During this time, the applicant should be informed:

➤ How long you expect the interview to last

➤ That you will be taking notes to help you remember his/her comments apart from other candidates

➤ That you will be working from notes to ensure you explore the requisite areas

➤ That you will ask questions first

➤ That you will provide an opportunity for the candidate to ask questions

It is always a good idea to close Step 1 by detailing the events of the day; for instance, the number of continuing interviews, with whom, and so on.

Step 2: Interviewer Q&A

As you ask your prepared questions, keep in mind that your objective is for the candidate to do most of the talking. A good rule of thumb is to keep the candidate talking 80% of the time.

If you allow the interviewee to assume control and get you to do most of the speaking, you will not learn much about the candidate. If you sense this happening, redirect the candidate with the following statement, "I know you have a lot of questions and I will be happy to answer them when I have completed my interview of you. For now, I need you to answer my questions." This will place control back into your hands until you have completed Step 2. As the candidate responds, be sure to note the behaviors and answers as detailed earlier.

The Interview Process (CONTINUED)

Step 3: Applicant Q&A

Most applicants want to show you they are interested in your company and the position. This is the point in the process for the applicant to request clarification responses and get a more in-depth feel for you and the company. This momentary "equal footing" humanizes both the interviewer and the interview process. Be prepared to deal with any number of questions and answer them as well as you can.

Step 4: Close

While the applicant is asking questions in Step 3, other questions to ask the interviewee may occur to you. This is the time to ask them. Step 4 is also the time to ask applicants if they have any final questions of you.

If you are confident that the applicant will make a good candidate for the position, Step 4 is the time to do a little "selling" on the benefits of working with your company. If, on the other hand, you do not feel this person is a good match for the position, you can begin the "dismissal" process by stating you will get back to the interviewee at a later date. This will be discussed more in the next chapter.

Step 5: Administrate

Do not wait until the next day to document the session. It is easy to confuse one candidate versus another even after one day of interviewing. Check your notes for consistency of response and behaviors and make a hire/no-hire decision based on the selected rating scale. Discuss your findings with others and decide how to follow up with the applicant. Consider whether you need to allocate more time, include other interviewers, script more specific questions, and so on.

Avoiding Interview Bias

There are four types of interview bias to consider as you rate the applicants. While we would all like to believe that we are impartial, it is difficult not to form early opinions based on what we see and hear. Any amount of bias could be problematic, so you must make specific effort to eliminate it.

Four Common Types of Bias

➤ Stereotyping

➤ Halos and Horns

➤ Comparison Error

➤ Initial Impression

Stereotyping

This is the assigning of attributes based upon assumed characteristics of a group of people. The grouping may be based on ethnicity, gender, or other cultural trait. Some people think Southerners are not very bright for no reason other than their accent. Likewise, when an interviewer asks, "How can you travel with young children at home?" that person is making a stereotypical assumption about parenthood. Placement decisions must be based solely upon *ability to do the job*; bias has no place in the interview.

Halos and Horns

These are opposites to avoid. Halos occur when the interviewer focuses on one piece of information and allows it to positively impact the entire interview. For example, the interviewer learns that the applicant is from the same high school or is a member of the same fraternity.

Horns will do just the opposite. An entire interview may be viewed as negative because, for example, if the interviewer dislikes facial hair or earrings on men.

Avoiding Interview Bias (CONTINUED)

Comparison Error

This one has been unflatteringly called "the cream of the crap syndrome." It usually happens after interviewing a number of people. If none of the applicants is impressive there is a tendency to think, "Well maybe the applicant I interviewed this morning was not that bad after all." The tendency is to force a placement decision, based on relative worth instead of documented skills and abilities. Avoid the tendency by *always* challenging your assumptions and by having multiple interviewers as a method of proofing all conclusions.

Initial Impression

Like Halos and Horns, this can be viewed from two perspectives: positive or negative. If a candidate is extremely well presented in dress and appearance, there can be a tendency to rationalize the "attractiveness" as "qualified." Likewise, someone presenting a negative initial impression may be instantly "disqualified." Let the interview *content* lead to a decision, not the initial first impression.

IDENTIFYING INTERVIEW BIAS

Recall past interviews you conducted. Identify any subjective thoughts you had of the applicant. List the attribute you assigned to them and then identify the type of bias this reflected. This exercise will help you become more aware of your biases and help you learn to focus on objective criteria in the future.

S=Stereotyping   **H**=Halos/Horns   **C**=Comparison Error   **I**=Initial Impression

Attribute   Bias

1. _____   _____

_____

2. _____   _____

_____

3. _____   _____

_____

4. _____   _____

_____

5. _____   _____

_____

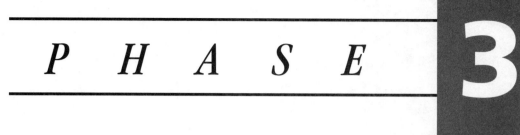

Interpret
Behavior

Interpreting Behavior

Interpretation of behavior is somewhat subjective. However, with the techniques you have learned in Phase 1 and Phase 2, you will significantly reduce the subjectivity of all your interviews because you focused on fact-based information. You will improve your chances of making a good selection further by keeping in mind that you are measuring responses to questions in two dimensions:

➤ **What you see**

➤ **What you hear**

As you observe and listen during the interview, keep the following in mind:

➤ Let the applicant do most of the talking. Generally speaking, the candidate should speak 80% of the time.

➤ Focus your complete attention on the applicant. This person deserves 100% of your time.

➤ Do not form instant judgments. Let the facts and the entire interview lead to a sound decision.

➤ Pay close attention to what is stated and how it is stated.

➤ Take notes to help you remember what was said.

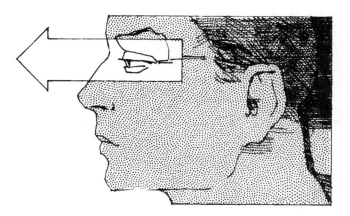

What You See

What you see is sometimes an eye opener. The interviewer should always focus attention on several informative areas: body language, eye contact, posture, facial expressions, dress, and grooming. Is the applicant reclining in the chair? Avoiding eye contact? Using little facial expression even when discussing a topic of extreme interest? Is the person neatly groomed and appropriately attired for the position of interest? Each as a single entity could be meaningless, but taken as a whole this could paint a picture for the interviewer.

For instance, if your profile dictates the need for a person with customer contact experience, you would expect at a minimum:

➤ Ability to communicate effectively

➤ Well-groomed

➤ Confidence with others

➤ A degree of assertiveness

➤ Ability to relate to strangers

Are any of the following behaviors in conflict with this criteria?

❑ Eyes cast downward a majority of the time

❑ Slouching in the chair

❑ Little or no facial expressions

❑ Arms crossed at the chest

❑ Hands gripping tightly to the arms of the chair

❑ Clothes wrinkled or some other disheveled look

These could be outward signs that the candidate:

➤ is non-assertive

➤ lacks personal grooming standards

➤ is nervous

➤ may not be comfortable in selling situations

➤ may not be comfortable dealing with people

If so, this is not an ideal person for a customer contact position.

Quiz: Evaluating What You See

If you were interviewing candidates for the job *you* currently have, what would you like to see in the applicant?

_____

_____

_____

_____

_____

Do you meet the requirements above?   ❏ yes   ❏ no

What You Hear

What you hear will confirm or raise additional questions about what you have seen. Here the interviewer will focus on style and confidence of presentation, vocabulary usage, voice inflection and intonation, stream of consciousness, and clarity of thought. Again, a deficiency in one area might not be a problem, but if a deficiency shows in several areas, the red flag should go up. Relating this to your customer contact position, did the applicant come across as:

➤ Confident or shy?

➤ Well-versed in the use of language and persuasiveness with it?

➤ Excited and enthusiastic?

➤ Able to think logically and speak in an organized way?

Quiz: Evaluating What You Hear

Think of your most recent interview. Rate the candidate on the following factors from 5 (great) to 1 (poor).

	Rating				
Style	5	4	3	2	1
Confidence	5	4	3	2	1
Vocabulary	5	4	3	2	1
Voice	5	4	3	2	1
Stream of consciousness	5	4	3	2	1
Clarity of thought	5	4	3	2	1

The Words and the Music

Simply stated, the "words and the music" are a combination of what you see and what you hear. For example, a person who claims to be assertive should be able to look you in the eye when answering your questions. A person who claims to have good interpersonal skills should not give indications that there was friction with former co-workers.

Putting the words and the music together will become second nature with time and practice. To increase your ability to combine what you see and what you hear to get an accurate picture of candidates:

➤ Make sure you base any judgment on all of the information presented by the candidate. A single bit of information is not enough to draw a conclusion.

➤ Look for repetition of behavior or comments, not isolated instances.

➤ Do not jump to conclusions. Let the information gathered in the interview point you in a direction.

➤ If something does not feel right, you are probably correct in your conclusion. Try not to rationalize observed behaviors or statements.

➤ Minimize initial impressions. Look for confirming or denying data in the interview.

In each of these areas, make sure you probe for additional information. That is, if a statement demands an additional question, make sure you ask it. Probe as deeply as you need to until you are satisfied with the response and can make a conclusion about what you have heard.

Do not judge a book by its cover: An individual may not "look" the part but could be excellent at the work tasks. If some inherent trait is there and you feel good about the person, you can always work on developmental needs later.

Quiz: Matching the Words to the Music

Think of the last interview you conducted. Where did the words and the music not match?

_____

_____

_____

_____

_____

_____

PHASE 4

Follow-Up

70

After the Interview

After all interviews are conducted, the interviewers should meet, compare notes, and make a hire/no-hire decision. Although this is generally the most difficult step of the process, it is not the last.

Checking References

Reference checking, for legal reasons, has become a difficult process. Many employers will not release any information other than name, position title, and in some instances, salary. This is for good reason, since lawsuits have been filed alleging that incorrect information prevented a person from getting another job. How can you still get the information you need? Here are four recommendations for checking references.

1 Get written approval

Your chances of getting the information you want are increased if you have the applicant's written approval to release any employment-related data.

2 Check discrimination laws

Discrimination laws apply to reference checking. *All* questions concerning age, religion, marital status, etc. should be avoided.

3 Maintain internal confidentiality

Keep tight control over the information obtained through reference checking. Limit availability of any findings to the human resources department and the hiring manager.

4 Leave reference checking to the experts

The human resources department should conduct the checks since they are more familiar with the do's and don'ts of the process.

The bottom line to reference checking:

➤ keep it professional—rely on experts

➤ do not stray from the boundaries imposed by discrimination laws

Letters of Importance

There are two letters to concern yourself with as you complete the interview process: the reject letter and the offer letter.

Reject Letter

If an applicant is not suited for the position, you must prepare and mail a *reject letter*. Never use postcards–this non-professional approach could eventually impact your ability to attract qualified applicants.

The most effective letter is one that is consistent from one applicant to another. Writing individualized, unique, letters is commendable, but it could lead to unintentional statements, promises, or other miscommunications. A signature from the human resource department or the hiring manager lends a personal touch to this form letter.

The reject letter is composed of three parts:

> **Opening**

> **Body**

> **Close**

Each section of a reject letter should be short and simple to reduce the risk of misunderstandings. Here is an example.

September 23, ___

Ms. Barbara Godden
1224 Hill Road
Sacramento, CA 95825

Dear Barbara:

(Opening) I wanted to personally thank you for taking the time to interview with XYZ, Inc. Those involved in the interview process wanted you to know they enjoyed speaking with you.

(Body) After careful review of your qualifications and comparing them with the requisite needs of the position, we find we cannot offer you employment at this time. We understand this is probably not the news you wanted, but we are confident you will find the right position for you.

(Close) We all wish you the best in your job search.

My best regards,

The intent of the reject letter is to:

➤ Present professionalism

➤ Come across as caring

➤ State the job fit is not there

➤ Be cordial at all times

The strength of the reject letter is that its neutrality can be used in any reject scenario.

The Offer Letter

The offer letter is always more enjoyable to send, but it, too, needs forethought and proper preparation. Like the reject letter, the offer letter also consists of three parts:

- ➤ **Opening**

- ➤ **Body**

- ➤ **Close**

However, unlike the reject letter, the offer letter can be considered a contract, so what you say and how you say it is very important.

When writing an offer letter:

- ➤ **Always state salary in monthly terms** to avoid the perception of a specified period of employment.

- ➤ **Use employment-at-will language** to ensure the applicant knows the employment is for no specified period of time. (If your company is governed by specific company contracts, or policy language or philosophy, or other binding statutes whether federal or state, this may not apply. Consult with your labor attorney.)

- ➤ **Adopt an offer philosophy:** "Lead with the best" or, "Save the best for last."

- ➤ **State any employment contingencies.** For example, explain if the offer is dependent on the candidate passing a pre-employment drug screen. (If your company is governed by specific company contracts, or policy language or philosophy, or other binding statutes whether federal or state this may not apply. Consult with your labor attorney.)

If your company's offer philosophy is to lead with the best—that is, to put your best offer on the table—make sure the candidate knows it. It will save needless negotiations. Sometimes it is better to give the applicant too much information rather than too little. If the person is interviewing with other companies, your chances of hiring the person are greater if you do not have any secrets or hidden agendas. Candidates will appreciate the honesty and professionalism of your organization.

Here is an example of an offer letter.

September 23, ___

Ms. Carol Borelli
7365 Hill Road
Dixon, CA 97898

Dear Carol:

First, let me tell you what a great pleasure it was having you visit us for interviews. We were pleased with the skills and talents you possess and would bring to our organization. As a result, we would like to extend to you an offer of employment.

Your position would be as our Director of Accounting and Finance. You would begin employment at a starting salary of $8,000 a month. You are bonus eligible but only if the company achieves its earnings projections and you meet any MBOs assigned to you. I will cover the specifics of the bonus program if you decide to accept this offer. As we discussed, we will arrange the shipment of your household goods for you.

This offer is contingent upon your passing a pre-employment drug test and we have made arrangements for one at (address). They can see you on Monday, October 4 at 9:00 A.M.

Finally, as we discussed, we are an at-will employer and as such reserve the right, as you do, to terminate the relationship at any time and for any reason.

If you have any questions, concerning this offer, please feel free to call at your convenience. We look forward to your answer.

My best regards,

This letter will also be viewed as cordial but will also generate some enthusiasm on the part of the candidate. This is the reason the letter starts and ends as it does—on a positive note.

COMPOSING AN OFFER LETTER

Using the offer format, write an offer letter based on the following scenario. David Bovill was interviewed for a research scientist position. He was more than qualified for the position and you wish to extend him an offer. He will have to move his family across the country if he accepts the position. His rate of pay will be $80,000 per year with the potential for a 20% bonus. Your company has an "at-will" employment clause and requires pre-employment drug screens.

Opening:

Body:

Close:

Did you remember to:

- ❏ State the salary in monthly terms?
- ❏ Describe the potential for bonus?
- ❏ State you are an at-will employer?
- ❏ Mention the pre-employment drug screen?
- ❏ Discuss the shipment of household goods and other perks?

Process Improvements

Every process needs periodic close examination. The interview process should be evaluated after each use and improved if necessary. It is always a good idea to ask yourself the following:

➤ Did we have enough interviewers?

➤ Did we have too many interviewers?

➤ Did the interview process take too long? If so, how can we streamline the process?

➤ Did we follow our process from start to finish?

➤ Did everyone involved in the process express positive feelings concerning it?

➤ If the candidate was lost to the competition or rejected our offer, why? What could have been done differently?

Examining successes and failures of the interview process will strengthen it over time, lead to a process free of legal concerns, and accomplish its ultimate goal—hiring the best person for the job.

Form Disposition

The question always arises, "What do I do with the completed forms?" Here are three suggestions:

1. Give all completed forms to the human resources department since they most likely control the selection interviewing process.

2. The human resource department should review each form for any sidebar (potentially damaging/discriminatory) comments. These should be clarified or eliminated.

3. The forms should remain on file for a period of two years. Generally speaking, if someone has a complaint about the process it will happen within this time frame.

A P P E N D I X A

200 BEHAVIOR-BASED INTERVIEW QUESTIONS

Behavior-Based Interviewing demonstrates how to develop selection questions. Here are 200 job-related questions to assist in assessing the behaviors and skills in twenty different dimensions. Notice, in keeping with the 80/20 rule, the questions are designed to keep the applicant talking.

Dimension: Time Management

The optimum use of time to maximize the results of self and others

1. Describe a time when a project under your direction was late and how you dealt with the issue.

2. Describe your current projects and how you keep them scheduled for on-time delivery.

3. Describe how you teach time management to those under your direction.

4. If a project is going to be late, what steps do you take to get it back on-line and on-time?

5. How many hours a day to you typically work?

6. What does a typical workday look like for you?

7. How do you prioritize your work?

Dimension: Risk Taking

Views failure as an opportunity for growth despite personal risk or exposure

8. Describe a situation where you heard of some new technology and implemented it.

9. Describe a situation where you were not supported in a task and how you dealt with it.

10. Do you think of yourself as an internal entrepreneur and why?

11. How do you determine if a plan is worth the risk of rocking the boat?

12. If it were apparent that there was little support for something you felt strongly about, would you try it anyway? Why?

13. What do you think of the phrase, "no risk, no reward"?

14. If you were not 100% sure about a (product/technology) viability, would you make a hire decision anyway and why?

15. Is there ever a time when a risk is just too big to take and why?

16. Describe a time when you weighed the pros and cons of a risk and why you decided to take it?

17. Describe a time when you were criticized for taking a risk. What was your reaction to the criticism?

18. Do you believe in the concept of calculated risk and what does it mean to you?

19. Describe a time when you seemed to be on the wrong side of an issue and what you did or did not do.

Dimension: Learning Ability/Capacity

The ability to absorb and adapt new technology to existing environment

20. Describe a time in your career where you heard of a new technology and how you learned the technology.

21. How many training courses have you attended over the last three years?

22. What were they? and

23. What did you learn?

24. Referring to those classes, what have you implemented as a result?

25. Tell which training classes you have taught and why?

26. Describe the various areas of your functional expertise.

27. This discipline is noted for its many tasks; describe all of them where you feel you have a comfort level.

28. Is there some technique or technology you want to learn but have not? Describe the situation.

29. In your last performance appraisal tell me what was detailed in the "developmental needs" section of the form.

30. In your last performance appraisal tell me what was detailed in the "employee strengths" section of the form.

Dimension: Decision Making

Ability to make timely/quality decisions not necessarily with all the information needed

31. Tell me your decision-making process.

32. What factors must be present for you to make a decision?

33. Describe an unpopular decision you had to make but made anyway.

34. Describe how you later kept selling the decision until it was applied.

35. Tell me about a time when you made the wrong decision. What went wrong?

36. Would you do it again knowing what you know now?

37. Describe a decision you made and came to regret and why?

38. Give me an example of a problem, issue, or concern that you handled in a unique creative way.

39. Do you ask for input before you make a decision?

40. Do you feel it necessary to ask others their opinion before you make a decision?

41. Give me examples of situations where you did feel it necessary to gather other opinions and why you felt it appropriate.

Dimension: Leadership

Demonstrating by example, the willingness to be out in front

42. How do you stay on the cutting edge of technology improvements?

43. Describe a time when you were in charge of a project and what you feel you accomplished.

44. Describe a time when someone reporting to you wasn't cutting it and what you did to rectify the situation.

45. If I asked someone about your leadership style, what do you think they would say about you?

46. If I asked someone about your management style, what do you think they would say about it?

47. How do you respond to the saying, "Leaders take hits"?

48. Tell me about the importance and value of workforce diversity.

49. Tell me about your affirmative action efforts within your group.

Dimension: Interpersonal Skills

Ability to relate/communicate/empathize with all organizational levels

50. How important is it to you to be liked and why?

51. Describe your predominant style with others.

52. How important is it to you to be perceived as a team member and why?

53. Describe a situation where you had to discipline someone and how you handled it with the person.

54. Describe a situation where you had to fire someone and how you handled the situation with the person.

55. If you heard through the grapevine that someone didn't care for you, what would you do, if anything?

56. Explain five interpersonal skills that best describe you.

57. What conditions must exist to create high morale?

58. How do you go about building relationships based upon trust and respect?

59. What would you do, or how would you deal, with someone you had heard was abusing drugs?

60. What would you do if someone stormed out of your office after a very negative review?

Dimension: Training of Others

Innate ability to teach or provide the skills required for task/mission achievement

61. How do you recognize skill deficiencies in those who report to you?

62. If a skill deficiency is not within your area of expertise, how do you teach the skill to an associate?

63. What is the process you use to uncover skill deficiencies in those who report to you?

64. Do you ever rely on those in your department to teach others, and if so why and/or why not?

65. Why is the concept of training and development important to you?

66. Describe a situation where you met with an employee on a performance related issue and what you did to resolve the issue.

67. Is there a one best way to approach the development of your team members or do you use a variety of techniques? Please explain.

68. Tell me about some of the people who were promoted as a result of your help and how you helped them.

69. If you were to leave your current position today, is someone ready to take your place? If not how are you preparing someone? If so, what process did you use to get someone ready?

70. Give me an example of a recent performance review where you detailed an employee's developmental needs and how you worked with the person to develop an improvement plan.

71. Tell me about some of the people you have worked with who later became successful as a result of your efforts.

Dimension: Training of Others (CONTINUED)

72. What were those efforts leading to his/her success?

73. Give me examples of how you have developed your staff to assume positions of greater responsibility.

74. How often do you review the performance of others under your direction and tell me about the topics you usually cover.

75. Tell me about someone who was promoted as a direct result of your development efforts. Why?

Dimension: Oral Presentation Skills

Ability to influence or present ideas logically through verbalization

76. How often are you required to present to groups? What are some of the topics?

77. How large was the largest audience you presented to?

78. Describe the preparation work you do prior to a presentation.

79. Have you ever been uncomfortable in front of a group? Why?

80. Describe the best presentation you ever gave and why you think it went so well.

81. How much prep work do you usually put into a very important presentation?

82. What are the essential ingredients of an effective presentation?

83. If you thought you needed assistance in planning a presentation, who would you turn to for help and why?

Dimension: Written Skills

Ability to influence or present ideas logically through a written format

84. How would you describe your ability to get your point across in a letter?

85. Describe a "letter to all employees" on a sensitive subject and what you wrote and how you wrote it.

86. What is the most challenging report you have ever written?

87. What made it so unique? and

88. To what audience was it written?

89. I've heard it said that one should write as if writing to an eighth grade audience. Is that your style? Why? Why not?

90. Is there a process you use to construct a letter? If so, describe it.

91. Describe your personality and how your writing style reflects that personality.

92. Describe the tone of most of your letters. Firm? Light? Why?

Dimension: Managing Change

Views and welcomes change as necessary for people and organizational growth

93. Tell me the part you played in implementing a new system and/or technology in your organization.

94. Tell me how you dealt with those who expressed the sentiment of, "Why change when we have always done it this way?"

95. Tell me about a time when you had to downsize/restructure the organization and/or department as it pertains to the process and how you dealt with those impacted.

96. Tell me about those left behind after the downsize/restructure. What did you do for them?

97. What new technologies are out there that you would like to implement. Why?

98. How do you win people over to the adoption of new techniques or technologies?

99. How do you instill ownership in people when new ways of doing things are introduced?

100. How do you change the culture of a business? Department? Function?

Dimension: Technical Skills

The requisite knowledge/expertise/skills for the task/function

101. Tell me about your expertise in (insert field).

102. I see you have worked with (insert technology). Tell me about its features and benefits.

103. What experience have you had working with (insert technology).

104. Give me examples of (insert technology) and how you adopted it for your last organization.

105. This position requires a variety of skills, describe your absolute strength areas applicable to the position.

106. Tell me how you stay current in your field on new or evolving (technologies or programs).

Dimension: Results Orientation

Delivers tasks/assignments on time, every time

107. Tell me about the goals you set for yourself last year and how you did toward achieving those goals.

108. Tell me about the goals you set with your associates and how you helped them achieve their goals.

109. Tell me about your goals for this coming year and your plans to achieve them.

110. Tell me about a project you are particularly proud of having been associated with and why.

111. Give me examples of projects you managed and how you kept everyone on track to successful completion of the project.

112. Describe your last set of MBOs (management by objectives) and how you accomplished them.

113. Give me an example of a goal you did not accomplish and what went wrong.

Dimension: Planning and Organization Skills

The skilled sectionalizing of tasks to optimize results

114. How do you prioritize your work assignment/projects?

115. When an unexpected project falls into your lap, tell me about the mental process you use to schedule it.

116. If you have a full plate and you are handed another project, how do you prioritize it given everything else that you have to do?

117. How do you respond to the statement, "Plan your work and work your plan?"

118. If you left your company today, what is left undone to your way of thinking?

Dimension: Delegation Skills

The assignment of tasks and objectives to others

119. How do you decide who gets what assignment at what time?

120. Tell me about a time when you delegated something that really needed your attention and why.

121. Tell me the advantages of delegation to you.

122. Tell me the advantages of delegation to the company.

123. Tell me the advantages of delegation to the employee.

124. Tell me about the criteria you use to delegate a project/assignment.

125. Tell me about a time when you delegated a project and the person did not want it. How did you handle the situation?

126. Give me an example of a major issue/crisis and the person you assigned to resolve the issue. Why did you choose that person? and

127. What was the end result?

Dimension: Coaching

Continual, constructive, ongoing feedback and advice

128. Explain to me the advantages of coaching.

129. How do you know when someone needs to be coached?

130. How do you know when to coach versus when to discipline?

131. How much time do you spend coaching each month?

132. Explain the thought process you use to set up a coaching session.

133. Tell me about your last coaching session. What happened?

134. How did it go?

135. What did you learn?

136. What would you change about the session?

137. What do you think the person learned as a result?

138. As a coach, tell me what you look for in selecting new team members for specialized tasks or assignments.

139. Tell me the process you use to integrate new employees into your area and with others.

140. What are the various benefits of giving performance related feedback?

141. What problems occur when feedback isn't sufficiently provided?

Dimension: Strategic Thinking

Continual assessment of the future for potential

142. Tell me about your input into your organization's last strategic plan.

143. What new and exciting technologies do you see on the horizon?

144. How do you stay in tune with new and emerging changes within your field?

145. Looking three to five years down the road, what changes do you see within your industry?

146. Tell me about a time when you went to the senior management of your company to detail a new technology (or development) that you felt your function needed.

147. Looking out five years, tell me the vision you have for your group.

Dimension: Mentoring

Guide and direct for the purpose of development/success

148. Tell me about a time when you took someone under your wing and what you tried to teach him/her.

149. What guidance and direction would you give to someone joining your organization?

150. Tell me about a time when you were mentored and how you think it helped your career.

151. In your opinion, what is the real value of mentoring?

152. Who should be charged with the responsibility of mentoring and why?

Dimension: Business Acumen

An understanding of the entire interconnectedness of business not just functional expertise

153. Tell me about your knowledge of other functions not related to your own. Describe in detail.

154. Do you have expertise in any other functions or disciplines? If so, describe.

155. How has your chief competition hurt your business?

156. If you could adopt something or some concept you know your chief competition has, what would that be?

157. Describe how functions within your business support each other to deliver what the customer wants.

158. Describe how international competition is impacting your business.

159. Describe how domestic competition is impacting your business.

160. What is the next big technological advance in your industry and how are you preparing for it?

161. Define the term "business partnering" for me.

Dimension: General Management/Thought Process Skills

Overall skills related and applied to organizational savvy

162. What does empowerment mean to you?

163. Two employees come to you with an issue. Tell me the process you use to manage the disagreement to a mutually acceptable conclusion.

164. What is your predominant management style? and

165. Why is it effective?

166. How important is empowerment in today's business?

167. Give me your thoughts on the value of empowerment.

168. What would you say to someone who wants your counsel but swears you to secrecy on content?

169. If someone comes to you alleging harassment by a co-worker, what would you do/say?

170. Is it possible to over-supervise and under what circumstances, if any, would you feel it necessary?

171. Describe a situation where delegation is not an option.

172. Walk me through a project you implemented. Who did you assign to the project and what were the skills they possessed that led you to put them on the team?

173. How often did you meet with those on your team?

174. If your department were experiencing trouble or bottlenecks with another department, what would you do?

175. Give me examples of methodologies you have changed or added to improve process flow.

Dimension: Customer Orientation

Understanding the importance of internal and external customer relations

176. Describe a situation where you had to go the extra mile to support an internal customer.

177. What was the reaction of the customer?

178. Describe a situation where you had to go the extra mile to support an external customer.

179. What was the reaction of the customer?

180. Do you believe the customer is always right and why or why not?

181. What is your process to handle customer complaints?

182. What is your opinion of having customers serve on a product development committee?

183. If a customer called you with a complaint, tell me your first reaction.

184. If a customer demanded a product you knew they really didn't need, would you provide it anyway?

185. Have you ever felt compelled to give your home telephone number to a customer?

186. Would you do it again and why?

Dimension: Problem Identification

The ability to discern issues creating difficult interpersonal or organizational situations

187. What is the mental process you use to make the determination that something is an issue and needs attention?

188. If you saw a problem in another area, especially one creating a bottleneck, what action would you take?

189. Choose a problematic issue from your own experience. How did you choose a person or team to resolve the issue?

190. Have you ever had a problem that needed only your attention? What was the issue and why did you take sole ownership of its resolution?

191. Describe a situation where you had to deal with a complex set of issues and how you resolved the issues.

192. Describe an out-of-control situation and the steps you took to resolve it.

193. Our company is non-union and we would like it to stay that way. What do you think a company has to do to remain non-union?

194. What steps should a company take to prevent sexual harassment?

195. What steps should a company take to prevent a hostile environment?

196. If you observed someone displaying inappropriate work behavior, what would you do?

197. Tell me about a time when your organization had to downsize or layoff and the part you played in the process.

198. What did you personally do to ease the transition for those impacted by the downsize/layoff decision?

199. Looking back on the downsize/layoff decision, was it a necessary move or could something have been done differently?

200. If someone were accused of some impropriety e.g., theft, what would you do?

A P P E N D I X B

Employee Requisition Form

Current and Future-Based Questionnaire

Interview Question Matrix

Interview Worksheet

Forms in Appendix B may be copied for individual use.

Employee Requisition Form

Position Title:_____   **Reports to:**_____

Salary Range:_____   **Date:**_____

❐ Additional Headcount
❐ Replacement
❐ Budget
❐ Non-Budgeted

Essential Duties: Detail key position requirements

Essential Qualifications: Detail education and experience

Replacement/Addition Justification: Detail the need for replacement at this time and funding

_____   _____   _____
Completed by   **Department/Function Head**   **Human Resources**

Current and Future-Based Questionnaire
Determining Additional Skills

Define the position's current management skill sets:

How will strategic and/or operating plans or conditions change or modify those skills?

Define the position's current technical skill sets:

How will strategic and/or operating plans or conditions change or modify those skills?

What factors make someone successful?

Will those factors change over time?

Are there any new and emerging technologies applicable to this position?

Interview Question Matrix

Dimension	Behavior-Based Findings	Potential Behavior

Interview Worksheet

Applicant's Name: _____

Interviewer's Name: _____

Position: _____

Date: _____

Note: Finalize notes/comments immediately following interview

Interview Worksheet

Behavior-Based Dimensions	Questions	Observable Behaviors/Notes

Rating:

❐ Acceptable   ❐ Acceptable with reservations   ❐ Unacceptable

Recommendations:

Additional Reading

Bailey, Mercedes. *Cliff Notes: Delivering a Winning Job Interview*. Foster City, CA: IDG Books-Cliffs Notes, 2000.

Beatty, Richard H. *The Interview Kit*. NY: John Wiley & Sons, 1995.

Deluca, Matthew J. *Best Answers to the 201 Most Frequently Asked Interview Questions*. NY: McGraw-Hill, 1997.

Eyler, David R. *Job Interviews That Mean Business*. NY: Random House, 1999.

Fein, Richard. *101 Dynamite Questions to Ask at Your Job Interview*. Manassas Park, VA: Impact Publications, 1996.

Hindle, Tim. *Essential Managers: Interviewing Skills*. NY: DK Publishing, 1999.

Maddux, Robert B. *Quality Interviewing*. Boston, MA: Thomson Learning/Course Technology, 1995.

Veruki, Peter. *The 250 Job Interview Questions You'll Most Likely Get Asked*. Holbrook, MA: Adams Media Corporation, 1999.

Visconti, Ron. *Effective Recruiting Strategies*. Boston, MA: Thomson Learning/Course Technology, 1992.

Wendover, Robert. *High Performance Hiring*. Boston, MA: Thomson Learning/Course Technology, 1991.

Yeager, Neil M. and Lee Hough. *Power Interviews*. NY: John Wiley & Sons, 1998.

NOTES

NOTES

Now Available From

Books•Videos•CD-ROMs•Computer-Based Training Products

If you enjoyed this book, we have great news for you. There are over 200 books available in the *Crisp Fifty-Minute™ Series*. For more information contact

Course Technology
25 Thomson Place
Boston, MA 02210
1-800-442-7477
www.courseilt.com

Subject Areas Include:

Management
Human Resources
Communication Skills
Personal Development
Sales/Marketing
Finance
Coaching and Mentoring
Customer Service/Quality
Small Business and Entrepreneurship
Training
Life Planning
Writing